Jake the Adjective

Written by Coert Voorhees
Illustrations by Powerhouse Animation

Meet the Parts of Speech

I name a specific person, place, thing, or idea. It's a big responsibility, naming things—a responsibility that requires a certain attention to detail.

Vinny the Action Verb

Some people say I'm all over the place. Some people call me a ball of energy. I take that as a compliment, because I just like to go, go, go!

I take the place of one or more Nouns or Pronouns. I always want the Noun's job, and I hang out with the Verb and Adjective.

I'm perfectly happy to link Nouns and Pronouns with the appropriate Adjectives, but it's not like I'm going to expend a lot of energy doing so.

I modify a Noun or Pronoun. I tell what kind, which one, how many, or how much. I pride myself on being the most artistic of the parts of speech.

Connie the Conjunction

Gather 'round everybody and let's have ourselves a wonderful time. I just love bringing words and groups of words together, don't you?

I modify a Verb, Adjective, or other Adverb. I tell how, when, where, to what extent, and under what condition. I often end in –ly, but I don't have to.

Izzy the Interjection

I express emotion!! Yep, I'm always here, always ready with my commas and exclamation points, just in case.

They call me Preposition because I'm pre-positioned. I'm first. At the front. Before every other word in the phrase? Got it?

I am a chameleon. A spy. An undercover operative. I infiltrate the sentence and act as whatever part of speech suits me.

JAKE THE ADJECTIVE

Graphic Design by Mckee Frazior
Printed by Friesens, Altona, Manitoba, Canada

This book is typeset in Komika Text

Distributed throughout the world by Ingram Publisher Services
www.ingrambook.com

Printed in Canada

One day, Jake the adjective offered to platypus-sit for Nelson.

The platypus was so fun to describe.

Platypus-sitting was tiring business, so Jake took a nap.
Have a good sleep, little guy.

Like all adjectives, Jake dreamed in color.
RED
COBALT
jade
gold
lavender

He didn't know how long he'd been asleep before
Nelson appeared at his window.
Jake, wake up!
Boddington is back!
Not again!

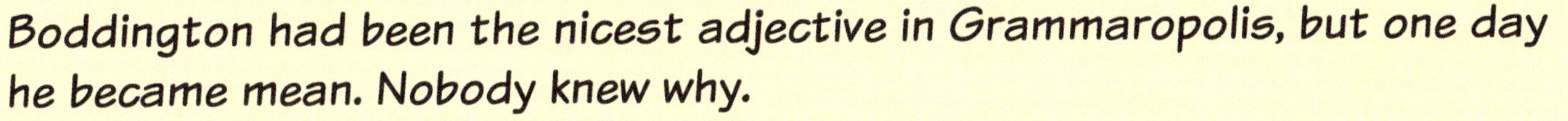

Boddington had been the nicest adjective in Grammaropolis, but one day he became mean. Nobody knew why.

This was Boddington's meanest stunt yet.
The last time he did something like this, I was just a baby adjective, an article.
You've got serious work to do.

Nelson and Jake soon realized that the situation was even worse than they'd thought.
He was leashed. Now he's gone.
By the way, where's my platypus?

Nelson was crestfallen, but Jake used some positive adjectives to make his friend feel better.
Try to be calm, patient, and hopeful.
We have to find him!
Then he and Nelson went to find the platypus.

There was no time to waste. Jake quickly restored the colors.

They saw Boddington had changed the description of the town river.
The trees are barren!
The river is dry!
The fish are scarce!

Jake modified everything back to the way it had been.
Platypus?
The tress are leafy and vibrant!
The fish are plentiful!
The river is full!

The town was a misshapen mess.
I can't get inside my house.
The walls are crooked and all the doors are circular.

Jake used adjectives of shape to change everything back.
Now the walls are straight and the doors are rectangular.
Is my platypus in there?

Boddington had changed the sizes of things.
What a huge, mammoth cat.
Did it eat my platypus?

So Jake used adjectives of size to modify them back.

Boddington had even modified the food.
Burger House
Are those burgers cold, bitter, rotten, and wooden?
Ew!
And nasty, bro.

So Jake changed that back, too.
Grammaropoli
Burger
House
Wicked yummy.
Yay!
How about warm, delicious, fresh, and nutritious?

Jake used comparative adjectives to show the degree of his description.
This jackhammer is quieter than it was before. And the street is smoother.
Thanks.

Jake even used a superlative adjective to restore the extreme quality of one of the buildings.
That should be the tallest one!
I hear something.

That's when they came upon a surprise.
Boddington! Why did you do all that!
I was lonely.
Platypus!

he truth was, Boddington didn't like being mean.
e just wanted attention.
I see that your friend is relieved and happy.
I missed you too, platypus.

Jake promised that Boddington would never be lonely again.
You're always welcome here.
Thank you. I'm so grateful.

Descriptions:
an
Adjective Journal

ADJECTIVES

An adjective modifies one or more nouns or pronouns.

MODIFYING A NOUN

My father is a brave man.

MODIFYING A PRONOUN

He is brave.

WHAT KIND

I only wear purple shoes on Tuesdays.

WHICH ONE

My cousin always sits in the front row.

HOW MUCH (QUANTITY)

Please give me more chocolate.

HOW MANY (AMOUNT)

I would like seven chocolate bars.

POSSESSIVE ADJECTIVES

A possessive adjective modifies a noun, showing possession or ownership.

That is my box of cereal!

Your dog accidentally ate his homework.

EXAMPLES

my

Your

his

DEMONSTRATIVE ADJECTIVES

A demonstrative adjective shows whether the noun it modifies is singular or plural and whether it is near or far.

EXAMPLES

this
that
these
those

INTERROGATIVE ADJECTIVES

An interrogative adjective modifies a noun and is used to ask a question.

EXAMPLES:

Which
What

COMPARATIVE ADJECTIVES

A comparative adjective is used to make a comparison between two nouns or pronouns.

EXAMPLES

taller
louder

SUPERLATIVE ADJECTIVES

A superlative adjective describes the extreme quality of something. It is used when talking about three or more nouns or pronouns.

EXAMPLES

tallest
loudest

ARTICLES (BABY ADJECTIVES)

The articles (a, an, and the) are the most frequently used adjectives. A and an are known as indefinite articles because they refer to a general noun (one that is not defined). The is a definite article because it refers to a specific noun.

EXAMPLES

a
an
the

CPSIA information can be obtained
at www.ICGtesting.com
Printed in the USA
BVHW050527110519
547997BV00001B/3/P

9 781644 420133